"Title To Go Here Please"

Please"

Bethany Humphries

BookLeaf
Publishing

India | USA | UK

Presentation by *BookLeaf Publishing*

Web: www.bookleafpub.com

E-mail: info@bookleafpub.com

ISBN: 9789358314632

First edition 2023

My Last First Poem

I thought of a clever and ingenious plan
To make me stand out from the rest
So I decided when I began
To make sure my first poem was the best

In order to achieve this feat
I thought I'd leave this poem till last
Then I'd know the poems I had to beat
To make sure this poem did surpasse

Alas I now wish I knew
When I left this poem till today
That I'd have nothing left to do
No funny words left to say

So though you'll read this poem first
Please note the rest have better themes
This poem was the last I versed
And should probably stay that way it seems

Past/Future Me

To Past Me:
Thanks for never wanting to be in the photo
And thanks for never being too outspoken
Thanks for never trying to do something new
Like singing or dancing, or other things kids do
Thanks for always being a quiet voice of reason
Thanks for staying steady in every season
Thanks for always trying to just fit in
Too afraid to rock the boat and get bitten

I don't have to worry about an embarrassing
memory
My history is coiled tightly like a noose around
me
I don't have to worry what other people think of
me
Because past me lived a life that was blissfully
empty

To Future Me:
Take the photo
Be outspoken
Do whatever you want to do
Be someone completely new

Bogeyman

It's weird the things that stick with us
That stay with us like a red wine stain
That hide like shadows in the abyss
In the hippocampus of our brain

These memories that lie asleep unheard
Unthought and thought entirely forgotten
Until someone utters a random word
And suddenly it's there in the flesh "begotten"

And we have no recollection
Of why we feel a certain way
Just the whisper of an emotion
A feeling we can't explain

I used to have a fear from an old home
About a haunted shed
I was too scared to talk about it
And it left me with a sense of dread

Then one day whilst reminiscing
About that home we used to own
I uttered a sentence, a forgotten memory
Of something I'd forgotten I'd always known

"Of course I didn't go into the shed"
"Because of the bogeyman living there"
Silence followed, as one would expect
What a silly notion I'd thought to share

I'd been only young at that home
My brothers much older and wiser than me
Who'd convinced their sister of a bogeyman
And she'd believed them, being only three

It did not matter that I was older now
Much wiser than my brothers had been
I'd carried that dread and fear around
Because of the bogeyman inside of me

Last Minute

I'm a constant deadline dangler
hanging on till the eleventh hour
And when crunch time finally hits
I surge on through with untold power

When I reach the final boiling point
And I find myself in a jam
No matter how terrifying the Dunkirk
I'll have a contingency plan

I'll scrape on through till the morning
In a last ditch effort to get the job done
I'll keep going past the last sunset
Right back into the morning sun

Whether you call them goals or deadlines
Milestones, or a target date
I'll always be deadline dangler
Holding on till it's just too late

Interlude

I made a haiku
Because I didn't know what
To write for today

Journeying

You wouldn't open a book
And start one chapter from the ending
Missing all the gory narrative
The bad guy, already apprehended

You wouldn't start a meal
Two thirds way through the main
Missing the starters and aperitifs
It would all sound quite insane

You wouldn't watch a film
That's 15 minutes from the credits
Trying to deduce the plot
Working out all its good merits

Don't try to start life in the middle
With all the hard work already done
You'll miss all the plots and narratives
Just take time and have all the fun

Don't worry about the journey
About some self-imposed limit on time
Start the book at the preface
Read it thoroughly line by line

If I Saw You

If I saw you in the street, I'm not sure I'd
recognise you
You'd probably have more wrinkles and more
grey hair too
You'd probably have a different smile and a
different point of view
You'd probably love me differently, not the way
I still love you

If I saw you in the street, I'm not sure I'd even
say hi
I'd probably turn the other way and hope you
walk on by
I'd probably try to sail on through with my head
held up high
I'd probably hope you don't see the tears I will
not cry

If I saw you in the street, I'm not sure what I
would do
You'd probably ask if I knew you
I'd probably say "I used to"

A poem from the heart

I thought I'd write a poem
Something from the heart
So I took mine out and placed it on the table
Ready for me to dissect
But the waiter asked me if I wouldn't mind
putting it back
As it was upsetting the other customers

Flowers

Dad buys mum flowers when he goes to the
local shop
They're usually the ones on offer that were
nearly ready for the final chop
He's never needed a special reason, to bring
them home to bloom
It's enough that mum loves them, that they
brighten up her room

Worst Fear

I always thought my worst fear
Would be of something quite mundane
But I wonder if my worst fear
Is that I don't know when I should be afraid

I jump and quiver at every thought
At every decision I have to make
I fear every conversation I have had
And every one I have to make

I am afraid of things I've said
And things I'm not even sure I've done
I enjoy the party at the time
But then fear I've had too much fun

Should I be afraid of what I'm doing
Should I fear the time that is to come
Should I worry about the closing darkness
Should I stress over the blinding sun

My worst fear, I think it's fair to say
Is the life I lead every day

Explaining Poetry

Sometimes poems are long
With good use of literary devices
And sometimes they are short
And they don't even rhyme

My Demise

On the event of my demise
I need to make it perfectly clear
I am not in some grave or urn
I will not still be here

On the event of my demise
It should be well understood
I was happy with the life I led
All the bad and some of the good

On the event of my demise
However untimely it may seem
I'm happy with where I am
Where I will be and where I've been

On the event of my demise
Don't wallow in self-pity
The crying doesn't suit your eyes
And the snot won't make you pretty

On the event of my demise
Know my love will always be with you
Like a lighthouse in the storm
Guiding your way through

On the event of demise
Keep living though I'm out of sight
And when you're in the dark times
My love will guide you through the night

Anger

Anger has this annoying way
Of being exceptionally unhelpful

Your hands tremor
Your eyes water
Your brain burns

There is no focus
No logic
No thought

Just
Anger

The Road

The road I take is mine alone
Though others may come into roam
I cannot follow another's line
Just follow the path that is all mine

The road I take is long and short
Others take roads of another sort
I follow mine from start to end
Through every straight and every bend

The road I take is sometimes sad
But I'll meet people who make me glad
I'll meet some people who maybe bad
But mostly they will all be mad

The road I take has no shortcut
And the ending may be a bit abrupt
I have no choice but to follow through
It is the road I must pursue

The road I take is mine alone
But I'd be glad for you to come and roam
We follow along like parallel lines
Never crossing your path over mine

Strength

Sometimes there are words
Filling each expectant silence

Sometimes there are silences
Filled with the promise of words

And sometimes there are no words or silence
Just two hearts beating

He holds her hand
No words or silence

Just the knowledge
He is there

Blissfully Average

Some people are destined for greatness
To reach the highest mountain top

But I get altitude sickness
And cramps in my legs on long walks

So I'll stick with being mediocre
Sailing along on level ground

Someone needs to be average
To make the rest of you look so grand

Lightyear

It's quite a tranquil thing
To see the sky at night
To see the planets and the stars
Shining up there oh so bright

It's quite a tranquil thing
To see the stars aglow
To know you're looking at them
As they were so long ago

It's quite a tranquil thing
To be so close to the past
To know a light can shine forever
Keep traveling on so fast

It's quite a tranquil thing
To think that when I'm gone
You'll look into the night sky
And my light will travel on

Modern Day

When all these young folk
Talk in their modern way
I shake my head and wonder
Was I like that in my day?

Then I remember
No, I wasn't
I was too pedantic for all that

Time Well Spent Haiku

If I spent as much
time living life as I did
writing this poem

I'd have lived very
Little of my life indeed
Because this is short

Poetical Punctuation

If you've noted the lack of punctuation…
In the poems you've read till now!
It's less to do with the subject matter,
And more because I don't know how;

So I'll make up for it in this poem'
Give different punctuation to each line)
Don't be bothered by the oddity(
I'll still ensure I make it rhyme*

My Last Poem

My Last Poem Should Be My Magnum Opus
My Greatest Masterpiece
But I Put Too Much Stock In The Rest Of Them
Alas This One's A Little Off Beat

I'll Redeem It With Capital Letters
With My Ballad Stanza Rhyme
And Hope It Gives You A Little Amusement
So You've Not Waste Your Time

Milton Keynes UK
Ingram Content Group UK Ltd.
UKHW021004070524
442340UK00016B/679